Creating a
Culture of Feedback

William M. Ferriter
Paul J. Cancellieri

Solution Tree | Press

555 North Morton Street
Bloomington, IN 47404
800.733.6786 (toll free) / 812.336.7700
FAX: 812.336.7790

email: info@SolutionTree.com
SolutionTree.com

Visit **go.SolutionTree.com/assessment** to download the free reproducibles in this book.

Printed in the United States of America

Library of Congress Control Number: 2016952634

Solution Tree
Jeffrey C. Jones, CEO
Edmund M. Ackerman, President

Solution Tree Press
President: Douglas M. Rife
Editorial Director: Tonya Maddox Cupp
Managing Production Editor: Caroline Weiss
Senior Editor: Amy Rubenstein
Copy Chief: Sarah Payne-Mills
Proofreader: Evie Madsen
Text Designer: Rian Anderson
Compositor: Laura Cox
Cover Designer: Laura Cox
Editorial Assistants: Jessi Finn and Kendra Slayton

Acknowledgments

Like all pieces of writing, *Creating a Culture of Feedback* is the product of a thousand conversations and shared experiences. For Bill, those conversations began with John Spencer, Scott McLeod, Dean Shareski, Paul Cancellieri, Julie Graber, Adam Garry, Amos Fodchuk, Lauren Hobbs, and Pernille Ripp. Each has, in its own way, challenged Bill's core notions about the fundamental shifts necessary for creating the learning spaces that students deserve. That's why he is so honored to have had the chance to write alongside them as a part of this Solution Tree series. Those conversations continued with Philip Cummings and Brett Clark—two friends who are always willing to polish Bill's thinking. Finally, Bill's work has been influenced by the teachers, principals, and coaches in the Burlington School District in Vermont and in the Fremont Unified School District in California, good people who have been thinking about student-involved assessment with him over the past several years.

For Paul, those conversations began with Erica Speaks, Luke Miles, and Justin Osterstrom. They pushed his thinking and created a sounding board for new ideas about grading, assessment, and feedback. Through continued discussions with courageous school leaders like John Bingham, Ian Solomon, Dhedra Lassiter, and Amy Walter, Paul has been able to build the confidence needed to enact change in his own classroom. He appreciated the support of his colleagues at Durant Road Middle School, Wake Young Men's Leadership Academy, and Rolesville Middle School in providing their own feedback about strategies and tools for providing feedback to students. Above all, Paul is enormously grateful to Bill for thoughtful guidance and patient support throughout the process of writing this book.

For both Bill and Paul, Diana Williams—an accomplished elementary school teacher from British Columbia—has been a tremendous help. Her willingness to translate concepts and practices originally designed for middle and high school classrooms into concepts and practices appropriate for upper elementary students have strengthened this text. What's more, her willingness to experiment with the practices highlighted in this text in her own classroom has proven that younger students *can* accept ownership over their own learning and that teachers of younger students *should* start incorporating student self-assessment into their regular instruction.

Finally, both Bill and Paul owe the staff of Solution Tree—particularly their editor Sarah Payne-Mills and Solution Tree Press President Douglas Rife—their deepest gratitude. Both have helped to shepherd this book from a rough first draft to a much-improved final copy that we are incredibly proud of and that we are convinced will help motivated teachers move from a culture of grading to a culture of feedback.

Solution Tree Press would like to thank the following reviewers:

Robert Blake
Director of Instruction,
    Curriculum, and Technology
Le Roy Central School District
Le Roy, New York

Hallie Edgerly
Science Teacher
Adel DeSoto Minburn Middle
    School
Adel, Iowa

Linda Marchineck
Coordinator, Curriculum
    Operations
Baltimore County Public Schools
Towson, Maryland

Nancy McDowell
Instructional Coach
Center Grove
    Middle School North
Greenwood, Indiana

Michael Podraza
Principal
East Greenwich High School
East Greenwich, Rhode Island

Katie White
Coordinator of Learning
North East School Division
Melfort, Saskatchewan, Canada

Visit **go.SolutionTree.com/assessment** to download the free reproducibles in this book.

Table of Contents

About the Authors

William M. Ferriter is a National Board Certified Teacher of sixth graders in a professional learning community (PLC) in North Carolina. He has designed professional development courses for educators across the United States. He is also a founding member and senior fellow of the Teacher Leaders Network and has served as teacher in residence at the Center for Teaching Quality.

An advocate for PLCs, student-centered learning spaces, improved teacher working conditions, and teacher leadership, Bill has represented educators on Capitol Hill and presented at state, national, and international conferences. He also has articles published in the *Journal for Staff Development*, *Educational Leadership*, *Phi Delta Kappan*, and *Threshold Magazine*.

Bill earned a bachelor of science and master of science in elementary education from the State University of New York at Geneseo.

To learn more about Bill's work, visit his blog *The Tempered Radical* (http://blog.williamferriter.com) or follow @plugusin on Twitter.

 **Paul J. Cancellieri** is a National Board Certified eighth-grade science teacher at Rolesville Middle School in Rolesville, North Carolina. He began his career as an educator in 2001 after spending several years as a science researcher. After ten years in the classroom, Paul spent a sabbatical leading the Data Literacy Program for the North Carolina Center for the Advancement of Teaching and returned to the classroom in 2014. He has worked at several middle schools in the greater Raleigh area, earning Teacher of the Year honors twice. Paul's focus is on grading and assessment, emphasizing best practices for fair and accurate measurement of student mastery.

Paul earned a Kenan Fellowship from the Kenan Fellows Program for Curriculum and Leadership Development in 2009 and works with the new fellows to improve their understanding of data and assessment. Paul is a member of the National Science Teachers Association and the North Carolina Science Teachers Association. He earned the latter's Outstanding Science Teacher of the Year award in 2012. He has been a member of the International Society for Technology in Education and the North Carolina Technology in Education Society. Paul has presented at the conferences for all four organizations, on topics ranging from progressive grading practices to practical ways to use tech tools for learning and assessment.

Paul earned a bachelor's degree in marine science from Southampton College, Long Island University and a master's degree in botany from North Carolina State University.

To learn more about Paul's work, visit his blog *Scripted Spontaneity* (www.scriptedspontaneity.com) or follow @mrscienceteach on Twitter.

To book William M. Ferriter or Paul J. Cancellieri for professional development, contact pd@SolutionTree.com.

Foreword

By William M. Ferriter

Can I ask you a tough question? How many students in your classrooms are truly satisfied with the learning spaces you have created for them? If your students reflect the national average, the answer is bound to be discouraging. Fewer than four in ten high schoolers report being engaged in their classes, and students often list boredom as the primary reason for dropping out of school (Busteed, 2013). Over 70 percent of students who don't graduate report having lost interest by ninth grade and, worse yet, the majority of dropouts are convinced that motivation is all that prevented them from earning a diploma (Azzam, 2007).

These numbers are troubling for anyone passionate about schools. They indicate systemic failure on the part of practitioners to inspire learners and warn us of the immediate need to transform education—a warning that school leadership expert and series contributor Scott McLeod (2014) issues:

> If we truly care about preparing kids for life and work success—*we need schools to be different*. If economic success increasingly means moving away from routine cognitive work, schools need to also move in that direction. If our analog, ink-on-paper information landscapes outside of school have been superseded by environments that are digital and online and hyperconnected and mobile, our information landscapes inside of school also should reflect those shifts. If our students' extracurricular learning opportunities often are richer and deeper than what they

experience in their formal educational settings, it is
time for us to catch up.

Scott is right, isn't he? Our schools really do need to catch up if they
are going to remain relevant in a world where learning is more important than schooling—and catching up can only start when we are willing to rethink everything. We need to push aside the current norms
defining education—that teachers are to govern, direct, and evaluate
student work; that mastering content detailed in predetermined cur-
ricula is the best indicator of student success; that assessment and
remediation are more important than feedback and reflection; that the
primary reason for investing in tools and technologies is to improve
on existing practices. It's time to implement notions that better reflect
the complexity of the world in which we live.

That is the origin of this series. It is my attempt to give a handful
of the most progressive educators that I know a forum for detailing
what they believe it will take to *make schools different*. Each book
encourages readers to question their core beliefs about what meaningful teaching and learning look like in action. More important, each
title provides readers with practical steps and strategies for reimagining their day-to-day practices. Here's your challenge: no matter how
unconventional these ideas, steps, and strategies may seem at first,
and no matter how uncomfortable they make you feel, find a way to
take action. There is no other way to create the learning spaces that
your students deserve.

Introduction
One Really Competitive Skill

Let's start with a simple truth: in a world where the Internet and the rapid pace of change have made remembering basic facts redundant and irrelevant, being career ready depends on a heck of a lot more than what a graduate *knows*. Instead, the most successful companies are interested in what their employees *can do* with nearly ubiquitous access to information and opportunities. They are looking for graduates who can think critically and solve complex problems that cross domains. They value ethical decision making, teamwork, and the ability to apply knowledge in real-world settings (Hart Research Associates, 2015). To the modern employer, adaptability combined with leadership, initiative, and strategic planning matter just as much as explicit knowledge (National Association of Colleges and Employers, 2014).

For most practitioners, there is nothing fundamentally surprising about these demands. Progressive educators have long pushed against the notion that mastering explicit knowledge determines success. The thinking of scholars like former Massachusetts Institute of Technology (MIT) mathematician, scientist, and educator Seymour Papert (1998), who reimagined learning spaces in the 1990s, predicted modern employers' expectations:

> So the model that says learn while you're at school, while you're young, the skills that you will apply during your lifetime is no longer tenable. The skills that you can learn when you're at school will not be applicable. They will be obsolete by the time you get into the workplace and need them, except for one skill. The one really competitive skill is the skill of being able to learn. It is the skill of being able not to give the right answer to questions about what you were taught in school, but to make the right response to situations that are outside the scope of what you were taught in school. We need to produce people who know how to act when they're faced with situations for which they were not specifically prepared.

So how do we better prepare students to master Papert's one really competitive skill? We must prioritize feedback over grading in our classrooms. Knowing how to act in situations for which you are not specifically prepared depends on the ability to gather and interpret information, to identify clear goals worth pursuing, to accurately describe headway (or lack thereof) made toward reaching those goals, and to successfully develop cogent plans for additional progress (Hattie, 2012a; Papert, 1998). Unlike grades—which are almost always formal, evaluative, and delivered by experts in positions of authority—the best feedback is objective, impartial, and delivered formally and informally by peers, parents or teachers, and the environment. While grades are designed to pass judgment, the goal of feedback is to serve as a fulcrum for continued growth.

Fortunately, educational researchers and experts have well defined strategies for using feedback as a fulcrum for continued growth. Perhaps most important, using feedback as a fulcrum for continued growth begins when classroom teachers make learning intentions and success criteria transparent to learners (Wiggins, 2012; Wiliam, 2011). As instructional experts Douglas Fisher and Nancy Frey (2014) detail in *Checking for Understanding*:

> A clearly articulated purpose provides teachers with guidance about checking for understanding and

> allows students to share responsibility for learning.
> When the purpose is not clear . . . students may
> complete a number of tasks yet not be motivated to
> assume responsibility. (Kindle location 215)

Using feedback as a fulcrum for continued growth also depends on teachers who provide students with information that is timely, targeted, and user friendly; who recognize that too much information can paralyze learners; and who understand that the best feedback suggests concrete actions that learners can take in order to move forward (Wiggins, 2012; Wiliam, 2011). As Grant Wiggins (2012) writes, "Even if feedback is specific and accurate in the eyes of experts or bystanders, it is not of much value if the user cannot understand it or is overwhelmed by it" (p. 14).

Teachers skillfully using feedback as a fulcrum for continued growth also empower students to lend each other a hand (Wiggins, 2012). They see potential in peer tutoring and recognize that the best way to demonstrate mastery of any content or skill is to try to teach it to someone else (Wiliam, 2011). As researcher, author, and professional development provider Dylan Wiliam (2011) writes:

> When students provide feedback to each other,
> they are forced to internalize the learning intentions
> and success criteria but in the context of someone
> else's work, which is much less emotionally charged.
> Activating students as learners for one another can,
> therefore, be seen as a stepping-stone to students
> becoming owners of their own learning. (Kindle loca-
> tion 2903)

Using feedback as a fulcrum for continued growth also depends on teachers who believe that students can actively participate in the assessment process. They understand that clear evidence of progress is the real source of motivation for any learner. As a result, they are committed to helping students see that they can achieve worthwhile goals one step at a time. They also create structures and processes that make it possible for students to track their own development throughout the school year. In classrooms where teachers prioritize feedback, students systematically reflect on what they already know and can do—and are continually looking for evidence that they *are* capable learners (Wiliam, 2011).

Rick Stiggins and Jan Chappuis (2005) of the Assessment Training Institute call this kind of work *student-involved classroom assessment*:

> Student-involved classroom assessment opens the assessment process and invites students in as partners, monitoring their own levels of achievement. Under the careful management of their teachers (who begin with a clear and appropriate vision of what they want their students to achieve), students are invited to play a role in defining the criteria by which their work will be judged. They learn to apply these criteria, identifying the strengths and weaknesses in their own practice work. In short, student-involved assessment helps learners see and understand our vision of their academic success. The result will be classrooms in which there are no surprises and no excuses. (p. 13)

The benefits of student-involved classroom assessment go far beyond simply helping students to see and understand *our* vision of *their* academic success, though. Student-involved classroom assessment rebuilds hope in the hearts and minds of struggling learners who rarely see evidence of their efforts and who, in traditional grading systems, feel task by task that they are failures compared to their more successful peers. By helping students spot the progress they *are* making toward mastering rigorous goals, teachers can create environments where everyone is motivated to learn (Stiggins & Chappuis, 2005).

But *is* that how your students view feedback? Are they eagerly using constructive criticism and meaningful praise to identify goals worth pursuing, describe the headway they are making, and develop cogent plans for additional progress? Or do they cringe whenever they receive feedback and respond almost reflexively with defensive phrases like "Yeah, but . . ." and "I tried that"? Are they willing and able to share meaningful feedback with their peers, or do they believe that all constructive criticism should be delivered from the "ones who know" to the "ones who don't know"? Are they *active learners*, convinced that asking the right questions about their own strengths and weaknesses is more important than finding the right answers, or have they become *passive students*, doing little more than working to master the facts in the required curriculum?

Sadly, there aren't enough students ready to forge ahead on their own. Crippled by the perception that feedback is something experts give, students are more likely to stand idly by, waiting for teachers to tell them what they know and what they don't know. Or worse, waiting to be told what they need to know and what they don't need to know and fighting against evidence of weaknesses, fearing the consequences that come with failure. Those reactions are a direct result of the long-held assumptions, habits, and beliefs that define assessment in traditional schools. By overemphasizing high-stakes evaluations as tools for reporting what students know and can do, we've created *a culture of grading* instead of *a culture of feedback* in our buildings (see table I.1, page 6). Spoken and unspoken messages that surround our students—lists of students who need remediation that rarely change regardless of content or classes, assemblies that celebrate final grades instead of student progress, and prestigious classes and clubs for honors students—reinforce the notion that success and self-worth are rewards reserved for those earning the highest marks on classroom assignments.

The good news is that it *is* possible to reimagine long-held assumptions, habits, and beliefs about grading and feedback. We *can* strike a healthy balance between using grades to report individual learners' progress over the course of a marking period and using feedback strategies that can turn our students into self-assured, self-directed learners who realize that having the know-how to move forward is always more important than being right in the moment.

Table I.1: A Culture of Grading Versus a Culture of Feedback

A Culture of Grading	A Culture of Feedback
The fear of receiving a bad grade motivates students.	The satisfaction of making real progress toward meaningful outcomes motivates students.
Students are disappointed when they don't earn As.	Students are rarely disappointed by their grades, recognizing that improvement is always possible.
Students are ranked and sorted by their academic ability. They are also aware of their own standing as compared to their peers.	Sorting only provides students with extra practice on outcomes that they are still working to master.
Students are embarrassed or ashamed when they struggle to learn a new concept.	Students are convinced that struggles to learn new concepts are nothing more than challenges to conquer.
Students are afraid that they might not be good enough to learn challenging content or to master challenging skills.	Students are hopeful and confident about their abilities to learn challenging content or to master challenging skills.
Students see feedback that the classroom teacher delivers as the final word on their performance.	Students see feedback, which they actively seek out on their own, as the starting point for new learning.
Students see grades as evaluations of learners.	Students see grades as evidence of learning.

Chapter Overviews

In *Creating a Culture of Feedback*, we will take a closer look at the role teachers in grades 3–12 can play in cultivating these skills and attitudes in their students. You will become more aware of just how important feedback is to developing learners, discover the characteristics of effective feedback, and explore a set of approachable instructional strategies for prioritizing feedback over grading in upper elementary, middle, and high school classrooms. The chapters draw on three commonsense questions that successful learners often ask and that form the foundation of research-based assessment *for* learning practices (Hattie, 2009; Sadler, 1998; Stiggins, Arter, Chappuis, & Chappuis, 2004): (1) Where am I going? (2) How am I doing? (3) What are my next steps?

Chapter 1: Where Am I Going?

Teachers who successfully prioritize feedback recognize that there is more to it than simply writing dozens of provocative comments and interesting questions on final copies of student assignments. In fact, the best feedback progressions begin long before students complete *any* work, as teachers help them identify outcomes worth mastering. This chapter examines the role that "I can" statements, unit overview sheets, and Not Yet / You Bet lists can play in bringing early clarity to the content and skills covered during an instructional cycle—a critical first step toward turning students into partners in the learning process.

Chapter 2: How Am I Doing?

Students need clarity about what mastery of complex tasks looks like in action. As a result, teachers who successfully prioritize feedback are constantly developing instructional strategies that ask students to compare their own work against authentic examples of accomplished performance. This chapter introduces the concept of *feeding forward*—providing students with enough information to learn to be right before they ever have the chance to get something wrong. You'll also learn about the role that High and Low Comparison, Revise It Once / Revise It Again, and Need to Have / Nice to Have activities can play in helping students reflect on the progress they are making as learners.

Chapter 3: What Are My Next Steps?

The most important steps in any feedback progression are those teachers take after instruction ends and they pass back papers. If our students are ever going to succeed at Papert's (1998) one really competitive skill—knowing how to act in situations for which they were not specifically prepared—they must learn to use feedback to independently identify logical and appropriate next steps worth taking. Chapter 3 examines the role that reflection checklists, unit analysis forms, feedback forms, and next steps reflection sheets can play in helping students do just that.

Integrating the techniques and strategies we discuss in *Creating a Culture of Feedback* into instruction will require additional time, energy, and effort, but like most meaningful and effective practices, they are worth it. Moreover, there are dozens of digital tools that can make these strategies more efficient for both teachers and students. Each chapter will highlight a handful of apps and programs that can supplement traditional pencil-and-paper techniques. Most carry no cost to educators and are easy to use.

The trouble with recommending online resources, of course, is that they change rapidly and can become obsolete or unavailable. As a remedy, we will maintain a constantly updated list of suggested tech tools at http://bit.ly/CCFtools to use as a reference for years to come. It will include the services mentioned in this book and any replacements or additions worth exploring.

Each chapter also includes sample handouts to structure more meaningful feedback experiences. These examples are shortened versions of the complete handouts to give you an idea of them in action. To further facilitate your efforts, we have provided you with ready access to customizable copies of the complete handouts. Visit http://bit.ly/CCFhandouts to access these editable, reproducible files. Our hope is that by having digital copies of editable files, you can begin changing your practices immediately. Visit the *Creating a Culture of Feedback* landing page at **go.SolutionTree.com/assessment** to download complete versions of the free online-only reproducibles in this book.

Conclusion

There really is no one right way to read this book. Maybe you will start at chapter 1 and work to the end of the text in order to get a complete sense for the kinds of feedback practices that you could implement throughout an instructional cycle. Perhaps you will read individual chapters addressing the specific feedback challenges that you are currently wrestling with or the technology recommendations that you are the most interested in. Regardless of how you tackle *Creating a Culture of Feedback*, find at least one strategy to use in your school or classroom. Changing perceptions about the role that feedback plays in the lives of successful learners may be the most important work that you do all year—and changing perceptions starts by changing your *practices*.

Chapter 1
Where Am I Going?

All too often, teachers use the terms *grading* and *feedback* interchangeably. We convince ourselves that any information we give students—letter grades on reports, number grades on quizzes, or written comments on projects—counts equally as forms of valuable feedback. The truth, however, is that grading and feedback are different practices serving different purposes and having different impacts on learners.

Grades communicate how well a student's work measures up against a teacher's expectations. Often given only after a student completes an assignment, grades rarely promote growth in learners. In fact, grades rarely even *report* growth. Instead, they boil down product, process, and progress indicators into one ambiguous number or letter (Guskey, 2009). The result is that students have no clue whether the grades they are earning are a reflection of the quality of the content they have created, the effort they invested into the task, or the fact that their final pieces were better than they expected. As Wiggins (2012) argues:

> The most ubiquitous form of evaluation, grading, is so much a part of the school landscape that we easily overlook its utter uselessness as actionable feedback. Grades are here to stay, no doubt—but that doesn't mean we should rely on them as a major source of feedback. (p. 16)

What makes grades even more useless as a form of actionable feedback is that they rarely surprise our students. Instead, because there's not much variability from task to task, grades do little more than reinforce perceptions that students already have about themselves as learners. For students accustomed to receiving high marks, earning good grades isn't rewarding. It's a relief. When you are an honor-roll student, anything less than an A or a B—regardless of what that A or B stands for—means you have failed. For students who never make the honor roll, each new graded assignment is just another opportunity to feel like a mediocre learner. Relying on grades as a major source of feedback, then, inadvertently creates a nearly inescapable intellectual caste system within our schools.

So what should meaningful feedback do? Wiliam (2011) explains it like this, "If I had to reduce all of the research on feedback into one simple overarching idea, at least for academic subjects in school, it would be this: feedback should cause thinking" (Kindle location 2592). In classrooms where teachers use feedback to cause thinking, students aren't just doing their work and waiting to find out whether their performance met grade-level expectations. The emphasis is on taking action, not receiving information. Our primary responsibility as classroom teachers, then, is to provide students with structured opportunities to think carefully about the work we ask them to do, to compare it against exemplars of success, and to draw conclusions about their own strengths and weaknesses based on it.

Defining Expectations

Ensuring that students understand exactly what is expected of them *before* learning begins is the first step toward using feedback to cause thinking. Students who clearly understand an instructional cycle's learning expectations can actively participate in the assessment process, measuring their own progress, identifying gaps in their own learning, and making corrections to their own course of action. Students with no real sense for the learning expectations, however, are "at best, just along for the ride" (Stiggins & Chappuis, 2005, p. 4). To help students understand where they are going, consider developing unit overview sheets and Not Yet / You Bet lists.

Unit Overview Sheets

Unit overview sheets are classroom handouts that clarify expectations for an instructional cycle by dividing the standards in the required curriculum into two broad categories: (1) *need to knows* and (2) *nice to knows*. While it may seem counterintuitive to suggest that some outcomes are more important than others in a required curriculum, it is simply impossible—for both teachers and students—to commit the same amount of time and energy to carefully tracking progress toward mastering *everything* listed in sets of state and local standards, pacing guides, and instructional materials. Focusing on five to eight essential standards for each unit creates the time and space necessary for moving from a culture of grading to a culture of feedback (Mattos, DuFour, DuFour, Eaker, & Many, 2016).

So how do you determine which standards to include on unit overview sheets? Start by asking yourself whether the knowledge or skills from the standard pass the endurance, leverage, and readiness test. Standards that have *endurance* help students master knowledge or skills that will be important long after they have left school; standards with *leverage* help students master knowledge or skills that they can apply across academic disciplines; and *readiness* standards help students master knowledge or skills essential for moving forward in an academic discipline (Reeves, 2002). Being persuasive, identifying bias, and using criteria to make judgments are examples of skills with both leverage and endurance. They are essential behaviors for success in countless classes and careers and will benefit learners working in any profession or specializing in any area of study. Mastering the conventions of standard English and reading on grade level with fluency and comprehension are readiness skills, necessary before a student can move forward in most language arts classes.

The next step in determining which standards to include on unit overview sheets is to think carefully about the unique needs of the students you serve. What patterns can you find in their performance over the past several years? Is there clear evidence of individual gaps in what they know and can do? Is there content in the required curriculum that has been covered in previous grade levels or will be covered in later grades? Does that repetition—often the result of efforts to spiral curriculum—influence instructional priorities? Regardless of the choices you make, remember that professional educators rely on more than just their intuition and instinct when identifying essential outcomes for a unit of study. Instead, they work systematically—and usually alongside colleagues who teach the same grade level or content area—in order to ensure that the priorities they are setting are truly *priorities*. The online-only reproducible "Identifying Essential Learning Targets" can help you to begin this work today. Visit **go.SolutionTree .com/assessment** for reproducible examples.

Once you have successfully identified a handful of essential learning targets for an individual unit of study, turn your priority list into an overview sheet that clearly communicates expectations to learners. The best unit overview sheets:

- **List essential learning targets in student-friendly language**—Curriculum-document language is rarely approachable for students. Try writing the unit overview sheet's essential learning targets in student-friendly language, which has been shown to improve learning by as much as 20 percent (Marzano, 2003). An "I can" statement is one strategy for rewriting objectives in student-friendly language. "I can" statements consist of two parts: (1) an opening phrase restating the required learning in age-appropriate vocabulary and (2) a specific task, sometimes called the *doing task*, that students can tackle to demonstrate mastery (Stiggins et al., 2004). For example, a complex social studies standard like, "Describe the role of the trans-Saharan caravan trade in the changing religious and cultural characteristics of West Africa and the influence of Islamic beliefs, ethics, and law," can be rewritten as, "I can describe how the Saharan caravan trade influenced the lives of people living in Western Africa. This means I can detail three specific examples of how the caravan trade led to changes in the cultures, religions, and laws of this region."

- **Include opportunities for students to rate their progress toward mastering essential learning targets**—Feedback becomes a fulcrum for continued growth only after learners recognize that there are always new content and skills to master and that making progress is possible. To facilitate these core beliefs, build opportunities for self-assessment into your unit overview sheets. Asking students to record their current level of mastery for each objective on a scale from one to five, on a number line, or on a rating bar running from "This is new to me" to "I've mastered this" can help students approach new learning with a clear sense of their own strengths and weaknesses in reference to the standards they are expected to master.

- **Provide students with space to track scores earned on traditional classroom assessments**—While grades should never be the primary tool for providing feedback in the modern schoolhouse, they *can* help students quickly spot gaps in their mastery of expected outcomes during an instructional cycle. Additionally, they *are* still widely accepted tools for communicating strengths and weaknesses to parents and practitioners working beyond the classroom. As a result, unit overview sheets often include places for students to track scores earned on classroom assignments. The key to using grades to support a culture of feedback is reminding students again and again that individual scores on unit overview sheets are *evidence of learning,* not *evaluations of learners.*

- **Provide students with space to record evidence that they are mastering required objectives**—Developing self-sufficiency and intellectual agency in learners depends on giving our students regular opportunities to demonstrate (to themselves, their teachers, their parents, and their peers) that they have mastered important concepts and skills. Encourage those behaviors by providing open space on unit overview sheets that students can fill with proof—thoughts, definitions, illustrations, sample problems, additional examples, and related questions—of new learning.

- **List essential academic vocabulary to teach during an instructional cycle**—For many students, mastering new words that appear again and again in classroom assignments and assessments can be the trickiest part of learning. If academic vocabulary plays a major role in the subject that you teach, remember to include a list of important terms at the end of your unit overview sheets, and ask students to check off any words they understand and can define. Doing so reminds students that sustained mastery of complex concepts depends on sustained fluency with discipline-specific terminology.

See figure 1.1 for a sample unit overview sheet.

For teachers in upper elementary, middle, or high school, listing all of the required objectives for one unit on the same document makes the most sense. That way, students can track their progress from beginning to end on the same handout. You can place unit overview sheets in a dedicated section of student notebooks or photocopy them on colored paper to make them easy to spot in messy binders and backpacks. For younger students, students with special needs, or English learners (ELs), consider turning each objective into a student learning card you can hand out one at a time.

Learning Target	Your Proof
1. I can explain how flowering plants survive and reproduce. This means I can correctly label the petals, sepals, stamens, anthers, and pistils on an illustration of a flower and detail the role that they plan in the survival and reproduction of flowers. This also means that I can explain how plants use dormancy and tropism to help them survive and thrive.	

Rate Your Level of Understanding			
1	2	3	4
Grades Earned			

Figure 1.1: Sample unit overview sheet.

*Visit **go.SolutionTree.com/assessment** for free reproducible versions of this figure.*

Doing so ensures that the number of objectives or overall length of a unit overview sheet doesn't overwhelm students. See figure 1.2 for a sample student learning card, and visit **go.SolutionTree.com /assessment** for reproducible examples.

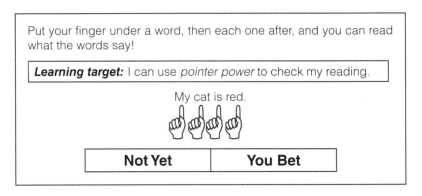

Figure 1.2: Sample student learning card.

*Visit **go.SolutionTree.com/assessment** for free reproducible versions of this figure.*

Remember, too, that the purpose of a unit overview sheet is simply to make intended outcomes for an instructional cycle transparent to students. If you teach by theme, story, or topic, you can easily rename the overview sheets to reflect that organizing strategy. Don't let the phrase *unit overview sheet* become a conceptual stumbling block. Don't let the specific format of a unit overview sheet become a conceptual stumbling block, either. The goal is to design a document that you believe in and that your students can understand easily. To help you get started, at **go.SolutionTree.com/assessment**, we've included three different reproducible examples of unit overview sheets. The first—"Unit Overview Sheet: The Scientific Method"—includes plenty of white space, which makes the content less intimidating and more approachable to learners. It includes an open-ended *proof box* where students can record evidence of their own progress toward mastery for each of the essential outcomes a unit of study covers. The second—"Unit Overview Sheet: Understanding Persuasive Text"—is designed to fit on one page. As a result, it has less white space and no places for students to record proof of their own learning outside of the grades they earned on classroom tasks. It does, however, include a *progress rating bar* that makes it easier for students to change their self-assessments over time. The third—"Unit Overview Sheet: Northern Europe"—is a simplified version of the previous examples, including a stripped-down rating system and eliminating features like essential questions and unit vocabulary in an attempt to keep students focused only on the learning targets for the current unit of study.

Once you have settled on a format and developed overview sheets for each unit in the required curriculum, integrate them into your daily work with students. Remember, after all, that the purpose of unit overview sheets is to give students opportunities to think carefully about the work you're asking them to do. Students should be using unit overview sheets at the following times.

- **At the beginning of every unit:** Set aside fifteen to twenty minutes at the start of a new instructional cycle for students to review the content they will be studying.

Ask them to set initial ratings for each learning target on the unit overview sheet. Then, ask students to share their ratings with one another, which will send the message that everyone has learning to do at the beginning of a unit, making it safe for students to share their struggles with their peers. It will also provide valuable information about what students know or don't know before instruction begins.

- **As frequently as possible during weekly lessons:** Consider asking students to pull out their unit overview sheets and review the progress they are making toward mastering the expected outcomes for daily lessons before you start teaching or at the end of every class period. Encourage them to reflect on what they know with a side partner or a trusted peer. Allow them to erase and change self-assessment ratings that no longer accurately represent what they know and can do. Ask them to find evidence—either in questions they answered in class, grades they earned on required tasks, or performances they completed during lessons—to support their new ratings. Spending five to ten minutes a few times a week changing ratings for individual objectives provides proof to every student that new learning is happening.

- **At the end of every unit:** In classrooms where students use unit overview sheets regularly, the last day of every instructional cycle becomes a celebration. Start by having students set final ratings for all the learning targets you expected them to master. Ask students to defend their ratings by answering questions about each learning target or by completing the *doing task* in each "I can" statement. Then, ask students to work with peers to reflect on the improvement they have made throughout the unit. Which learning targets did they make the most growth on? Which learning targets are they the proudest of mastering? Where do they still have a bit of learning left to do?

Whatever you do, don't skip opportunities for students to have conversations about their learning and growth. Those conversations reinforce the notion that monitoring progress is the learner's responsibility, not the teacher's, and send the message that every student—regardless of the grades he or she is used to making—is capable of learning (Hattie, 2012a). Both messages define classrooms that have moved away from a culture of grading and toward a culture of feedback.

Not Yet / You Bet Lists

As with unit overview sheets, students use Not Yet / You Bet lists to track their progress toward mastering essential content and skills during an instructional cycle. At the beginning of a unit, share lists of important outcomes with your class. Chances are that after initial conversations and moments of reflection with side partners, students will add most of these outcomes to the Not Yet column of their Not Yet / You Bet list. Then, as students collect evidence of new learning, they can move content listed in the Not Yet column into the You Bet column. The physical act of moving content on Not Yet / You Bet lists reminds students that they *are* making progress and that they *can* learn—important messages for building confident, self-directed learners. See figure 1.3 for an example.

Not Yet	You Bet
Content or skills I am still working to master.	Content or skills I have already mastered.
☐ _____	☐ _____
☐ _____	☐ _____
☐ _____	☐ _____

Reflection Questions

1. Rank the items on your Not Yet list from the most important to master to the least important to master. Why did you rank them this way?

2. Which items on your Not Yet list are you the closest to mastering? What steps could you take today to move even closer to mastering those items?

3. List some of the strategies you used to master the items on your You Bet list. Do you see any patterns in the strategies that typically help you master new content or skills? Can you apply any of those strategies to mastering the items in your Not Yet list?

Figure 1.3: Sample Not Yet / You Bet list.

*Visit **go.SolutionTree.com/assessment** for a free reproducible version of this figure.*

Not Yet / You Bet lists have value beyond the classroom too. They are simple tools that students—whether they are baseball players, gymnasts, pianists, or martial artists—can use to detail their progress toward their personal interests and passions. At the beginning of each new season, parents, coaches, or tutors can help students generate a list of skills worth working on. After practices, training sessions, or recitals, students can revisit their Not Yet / You Bet lists to reflect on their progress. By asking students to think carefully about their own strengths and weaknesses in learning situations outside school, Not Yet / You Bet lists can reinforce the notion that actively monitoring individual progress isn't just a school skill. It's a life skill.

Using Digital Tools to Help Students Understand Where They Are Going

For many teachers and learning teams, bringing clarity to the expected outcomes of individual lessons or units of study begins by working with *other practitioners* to rewrite curriculum standards in student-friendly language and to share that content on unit overview sheets or student learning cards. But what if we asked *students* to rewrite curriculum standards in more approachable language? Wouldn't learners benefit from firsthand experiences wrestling with the language in the standards we expect them to master?

A great way to facilitate this work is to ask students to analyze essential standards using the Readability Test Tool (www.webpagefx .com/tools/read-able)—a simple website that ranks the readability of any selection of text on a grade-level scale. It is free to use and doesn't require an account or login. Best of all, the results are easy to understand. Students using the Readability Test Tool can identify the factors—average number of syllables per word, average number of words per sentence, and percentage of complex words across an entire selection—influencing an individual standard's readability, allowing for targeted revisions to make the text more approachable. Students using the Readability Test Tool can also test the readability of any standard they rewrite to ensure their classmates can understand their final statements.

Another way to help make expected outcomes clearer is to have students use summarizing tools like Tagxedo (www.tagxedo.com) and Wordle (www.wordle.net) to identify the big ideas and essential vocabulary words in sets of learning standards. Using either tool, students can paste a string of text from any source—think objectives or introductory narratives from district curriculum guides—to generate a visual "cloud" of words (see figure 1.4). The cloud displays the words in a font size proportional to their relative use, so the more often a word occurs in the text, the larger it appears. Both tools allow users to export the resulting word clouds as image files, which teachers can then integrate into unit overview sheets as a constant visual cue of the concepts that matter the most in the current unit of study.

Finally, involve students in the collaborative construction of essential learning targets or the identification of big ideas with Padlet (www.padlet.com). This tool encourages users to contribute to an online bulletin board by pinning individual items that they can

Figure 1.4: Sample word cloud.

manually arrange or place automatically in a constantly developing stream of ideas. The items, which resemble sticky notes, can contain a title and text, images, or files. Anyone with a link can view and edit the board, which makes it possible for students to contribute without needing usernames or passwords. Have students add critical questions, important vocabulary, or rewritten essential learning targets to developing Padlets when each unit begins. Then, ask students to review the targets or vocabulary their own peers have added to a developing Padlet. Doing so can reinforce—or transparently challenge—a learner's personal interpretations of the expected outcomes. When finished, you or students can manage, group, or merge Padlet responses in a common space visible to all. For an example, visit http://bit.ly/CCFpadletsample for the Padlet "What Will We Learn in the Natural Resources Unit?" No matter how you involve students in setting targets, it is important that they engage with the standards so that learning begins with a clear sense of the content to be covered.

Conclusion

What comes to mind when you think of the modern workplace? Do you think of steady positions that rarely change from year to year, where the skills employees possess when hired are the same skills they will use when they retire? Or do you think of constantly changing environments where new challenges—for employees and their employers—are the norm? Are you convinced that Papert (1998) was correct to argue that making "the right response to situations that are outside the scope of what you were taught in school" is the one truly competitive skill that students need to master before graduation?

If so, then students need to accept responsibility for monitoring their *own* strengths and weaknesses—a responsibility often stripped away in traditional schools where assessment still means that experts evaluate progress. Helping students shift from a culture of "being evaluated" to a culture of "evaluating myself" is essential to developing the skills and dispositions necessary for making the right response in unpredictable situations—and it begins with transparent, approachable expectations for each instructional cycle. Students must also become skilled at identifying worthy outcomes even if experts don't clearly define those outcomes in advance. Finally, they must become skilled at tracking their progress toward mastery—and must put as much faith in their own assessments of progress as they do in the assessments made by people in positions of authority.

Whether you develop unit overview sheets or student learning cards detailing the essential knowledge and skills covered in every unit, encourage students to use Not Yet / You Bet lists to track their progress as learners in school or at home, or use digital tools to help students spot the patterns in the curriculum's expectations, concentrate on giving students multiple opportunities to better understand both themselves and the outcomes you are expecting them to master. Doing so will help students think carefully about the work you are asking them to do before that work even begins.

Chapter 2
How Am I Doing?

Whether feedback occurs in the workplace or in the classroom, it has almost always flows downhill. Managers use feedback as a tool for evaluating employees and for reinforcing the organization's goals. Annual reviews summarize an employee's strengths and weaknesses—and compare an employee's performance against the performance of their peers (Goldsmith, 2002). Traditional schools have mimicked this flow: teachers most frequently use feedback as a tool to critique and assess student performance against grade-level standards. Those critiques and assessments then determine the grades students earn, which become the de facto sorting tools for rating and ranking learners. In both circumstances, the primary purpose of feedback isn't to improve a learner's performance. It is to justify an authority figure's evaluations. The result is discouraging: feedback is rarely helpful *or* hopeful, leaving learners with little more than lists of ways that they haven't met expectations.

For noted executive coach Marshall Goldsmith (2002), the solution is to prioritize *feedforward*—information that can help learners better understand future expectations and identify next steps—over *feedback* in our organizations:

> There is a fundamental problem with all types of feedback: it focuses on the past, on what has already occurred—not on the infinite variety of opportunities

that can happen in the future. As such, feedback can
be limited and static, as opposed to expansive and
dynamic. . . . Feedforward helps people envision and
focus on a positive future, not a failed past.

Feedforward is built on the belief that everyone has the innate
desire and ability to succeed. Delivered *before* important work even
begins, the goal of feedforward isn't to evaluate learners' performance
at all. Instead, the goal is to better define the skills and competencies
necessary to successfully tackle the task at hand (Goldsmith, 2002).
Feedforward opportunities remind everyone that clarity is an essential prerequisite for competent performance. Learners walk away
from feedforward experiences energized, empowered, and armed
with a better sense of what they need to know and be able to do in
order to meet—and even *exceed*—expectations.

Using Feedforward in the Classroom

In many ways, Goldsmith's (2002) notion of feedforward is essential for helping students to develop Papert's (1998) one really competitive skill: knowing how to act in situations for which they are
not specifically prepared. Identifying clear goals worth pursuing,
accurately describing the headway (or lack thereof) made toward
reaching those goals, and articulating cogent plans for moving forward are action-oriented tasks dependent on learners who are convinced that they have what it takes to accomplish anything. Building
that confidence in your classroom means giving students opportunities to compare their own efforts and expectations against exemplars
of success before, during, and after the creative process. A few simple
techniques to develop these competencies in students are High and
Low Comparison, Revise It Once / Revise It Again, and Need to
Have / Nice to Have activities.

What makes High and Low Comparison, Revise It Once / Revise
It Again, and Need to Have / Nice to Have activities unique
is that the teacher doesn't provide direct feedback to students at

all—students almost always complete these tasks before they turn in final products. Feedback comes in the form of observations students make and conclusions they draw while individually and collectively examining examples of high-quality work. Teachers who embrace High and Low Comparison, Revise It Once / Revise It Again, and Need to Have / Nice to Have activities remind their students that the best feedback is actively gathered rather than passively received and that the best learners are always looking to explore examples of accomplishment.

High and Low Comparison

rubrics?

High and Low Comparison tasks present students with three to five essential criteria for a successful performance on a required assignment that are written in short, approachable phrases based on *observable* traits. Vague descriptors like "Piece is well written and includes elaboration" are replaced with more specific descriptions of success like "Quotes from experts elaborate key points in each paragraph."

High and Low Comparison tasks also present students with two exemplars of success. One exemplar models a high level of student mastery while the other models a low level of student mastery. Working alone, students use a feedback grid (Wiliam, 2011) to record the success criteria from both exemplars, determine which example represents accomplished performance, and compare their own work to the sample work.

Finally, High and Low Comparison tasks ask students to compare their ratings of each exemplar with the ratings their peers give them, and together they look for specific points of agreement or disagreement. Side-by-side partners defend their ratings by referring to evidence spotted in the exemplars. See figure 2.1 (page 28) for an example.

High and Low Comparison Task: Paper Towel Lab Conclusions

A good conclusion to a science lab accomplishes four different things.

1. Summarizes your findings
2. Reflects on any surprising results
3. Shares lessons that people can learn from your findings
4. Designs a follow-up experiment answering a new and interesting question related to your topic

Knowing that, explain why conclusion 1 is better than conclusion 2.

Conclusion 1	Conclusion 2
The paper towel that held the least amount of water was the one that was folded into eighths. It held 34.3 mL of water. The paper towel that held the most water was the regular paper towel that had nothing done to it. It held 41 mL of water. I thought this was very interesting because . . .	One of the things that we learned in our lab trials was that a paper towel that is folded doesn't absorb as much water as one that is used in one flat sheet. This was surprising to me because I thought that anytime you use more layers of paper towel, you could absorb more water. This was surprising because . . .

Feedback Grid				
Conclusion You Are Studying	**Summarizes Your Findings**	**Reflects on Surprising Results**	**Shares Lessons Learned From Findings**	**Designs Follow-Up Experiment**
Conclusion 1				
Conclusion 2				
My Conclusion				

Source: Adapted from Wiliam, 2011.

Figure 2.1: Sample High and Low Comparison task.

*Visit **go.SolutionTree.com/assessment** for a free reproducible version of this figure.*

Revise It Once / Revise It Again

Revise It Once / Revise It Again activities highlight sample responses to classroom tasks that have been systematically revised and improved. Students start by studying each example and identifying specific changes made from version to version. Then, students summarize the ways that each revision improved the final product. Finally, students spot opportunities in their own work for making similar revisions to their original attempts. See figure 2.2 for an example.

Revise It Once / Revise It Again Activity: Paper Towel Lab Reflection Sheet

Take a look at the following sample reflection statement. How does it improve from one revision to the next? Decide which reflection statements resemble the kinds of statements you included in your final product. Then, find one statement in your conclusion that you can improve and improve it through revision.

Original Statement	Revise It Once	Revise It Again
Our hypothesis wasn't correct, because folding a paper towel didn't make it more absorbent.	Our group thought that folding a paper towel would make it more absorbent because a folded paper towel has more layers than a flat paper towel. Our results showed, however, that folded paper towels do not absorb more water than flat paper towels.	After learning that a flat paper towel can absorb 23 mL of water, our group made a prediction that a folded paper towel could absorb at least 30 mL of water. Our thinking was . . .

What kinds of changes did you make from revision to revision? Do those changes improve the statement? Why or why not? If you had to draw a conclusion about a simple way to improve your reflection statements, what would it be?

One simple way to improve my reflection statements is to:

This improves my final product because:

Your Turn

Your Original Reflection Statement	Revise It Once	Revise It Again

Figure 2.2: Sample Revise It Once / Revise It Again activity.

*Visit **go.SolutionTree.com/assessment** for a free reproducible version of this figure.*

The key to successful Revise It Once / Revise It Again activities is to use examples that highlight one or two tangible steps students can take to improve their final products. For example, the revisions in the Revise It Once / Revise It Again reproducible at **go.SolutionTree .com/assessment**, all center on incorporating data into reflection statements for a lab report. By focusing attention on one or two tangible steps, students are more likely to actually *use* the lessons they learned from comparing their work against exemplars of success—an important characteristic of meaningful feedback. As Jan Chappuis (2012) argues:

> Students differ in their capacity for responding to cor-
> rection, and too much corrective feedback at one time
> can cause a student to shut down, guaranteeing that
> no further learning will take place. In such cases, con-
> sider letting go of the urge to provide all correctives
> necessary to make the work perfect and instead pro-
> vide as much guidance as the student can reasonably
> act on. (p. 39)

In both High and Low Comparison tasks and Revise It Once / Revise It Again activities, teachers share the characteristics of high-quality work with students in advance. This way, novice learners benefit from teachers' expertise when comparing their work against exemplars of success, and teachers can explicitly focus student attention on expectations in the required curriculum. But how do you avoid entirely stripping away the valuable learning experience of working with an exemplar to independently identify the essential criteria for a product or a performance? That's where the Need to Have / Nice to Have activities come in.

Need to Have / Nice to Have

Inspired by Jennifer Brouhard's Keep It or Junk It vocabulary strategy (Slattery & Weimberg, 2012), Need to Have / Nice to Have activities ask students to work alone to review an exemplar of success and to record the traits they believe have a positive impact on the final product. Then, students generate a ranked list of three criteria that define success. Sometimes, individual reflections become stand-alone statements of essential criteria. For example, "This piece includes lots of elaboration" on a Need to Have / Nice to Have activity designed to set criteria for a persuasive essay can become "High-quality persuasive pieces always include lots of elaboration sentences." Other times, one criterion can combine two or more individual reflections. Statements like "The author has no spelling errors" and "Every sentence has the proper punctuation" can become "High-quality persuasive pieces always have strong writing conventions." It is even possible that students will completely leave off individual reflections from their lists of essential criteria because they weren't important enough to include.

After students generate their own rank-ordered lists of essential criteria, assign them to small groups to look for patterns in their initial observations. The group considers each member's unique characteristic of high-quality work and sorts it into one of four categories.

1. **Need to Haves:** Traits that are absolutely essential to a high-quality final product

2. **Nice to Haves:** Traits that often appear in high-quality final products but are not absolutely essential

3. **Not Necessary:** Traits that rarely appear in high-quality final products

4. **Not Sure:** Traits that the group can't come to consensus around

Finally, each group shares its Need to Haves list with the entire class. Groups select the traits that appear the most frequently for inclusion on a class rubric or checklist that students can use to monitor progress on both first drafts and final products. See figure 2.3 (page 32) for an example.

**Need to Have / Nice to Have Activity:
Criteria for a Good Persuasive Essay**

Over the next week, you will be writing a persuasive essay in class. To prepare for that essay, follow these steps to identify the essential criteria found in high-quality persuasive pieces.

Step 1: Read and Reflect on Your Own

Working by yourself, read the following persuasive essay. While reading, record things that make it a strong piece of persuasive writing.

Text	What Makes This a Strong Piece of Writing?
It's officially that time of year again, when students are going back to school, and the school lunch debates are taking the news by storm. According to a U.S. News report, over thirty-two million students take advantage of the school lunch program, and twelve million use the breakfast program. But since 2010, government officials have been remodeling the school lunch program by adding more fresh fruits and veggies, providing low-fat or fat-free milk, reducing the amount of sodium in the products and ingredients they use, and slowly converting all the grains to whole grains (Taub-Dix, 2014). But how . . .	

Step 2: List Three Criteria of a Strong Piece of Persuasive Writing

Working by yourself, decide on the top-three criteria that you think we should use to judge persuasive essays. What characteristics will we find in the best persuasive essays? Why are those characteristics so important?

Criteria That Matter	Reasons I Believe These Criteria Matter

Step 3: Identify Need to Have / Nice to Have Criteria

Working with partners, review the criteria that you thought were essential for judging persuasive essays. Together, sort your shared criteria into four categories: (1) Need to Haves, (2) Nice to Haves, (3) Not Necessary, and

(4) Not Sure. Remember that we will be using your lists to build our class rubric for persuasive essays.

Persuasive Essays Need to Have:	It Would Be Nice if Persuasive Essays Had:
It Is Not Necessary for Persuasive Essays To:	**We Are Not Sure if Persuasive Essays Should:**

Step 4: Share Your Criteria With Our Class

Now we will work as a class to share our essential criteria for a good persuasive essay. We will:

- Record each group's criteria
- Look for criteria that appear on multiple lists
- Allow people to argue for criteria that don't appear on multiple lists
- Decide on three criteria to include on our persuasive essay rubric

Remember to speak up if you think that important criteria are being left off of our rubric!

Source: Cohen, Richardson, Parker, Catalano, & Rimm, 2014; Taub-Dix, 2014.

Figure 2.3: Sample Need to Have / Nice to Have activity.

Visit go.SolutionTree.com/assessment for a free reproducible version of this figure.

Using Digital Tools to Help Students Understand How They Are Doing

By asking students to look closely at sample work early during an instructional cycle, teachers are using feedforward strategies to prove that it is possible to succeed. But for exemplars of success to be worthwhile, students need to use them for more than just making comparisons. Instead, experiences with exemplars must lead to action. Digital tools can help by removing the traditional obstacles that discourage students from refining the content they are creating. Stated more simply, when revision based on exemplars is easy, students are more likely to persistently improve their work.

For many teachers, making it easier for students to take action after comparing their work against established standards starts by distributing templates and exemplars through Google Docs (http://docs.google.com) and Google Classroom (http://classroom.google.com). Google Docs is an online word processor that allows students and teachers to create and share documents with one another. Teachers can make virtual handouts that students complete online, saving both paper and time. Taken a step further, teachers and classmates can add comments and suggest edits directly on shared Google Docs, allowing authors to revise without having to rewrite entire sections of their original text. You can also use Google Docs to create templates outlining the format for upcoming writing assignments and including sample sentences for students to examine. Students can open the templates electronically, review the expected format and examples, and create their own original content. Providing exemplars directly on a document that can be easily edited scaffolds the work for students—and scaffolding work is a key step for moving learners forward.

Google Classroom, which is available only in districts that have embraced Google Apps for Education (www.google.com/edu/products/productivity-tools), enhances the use of Google Docs in lots of meaningful ways. Perhaps most important, teachers can distribute copies of classroom templates to every student, and every student can submit completed work to their teacher with the click of a button. Teachers can then respond to submitted work from a streamlined dashboard, making it possible to review many items quickly while still providing meaningful feedback.

Newer tools act as add-ons to Google Docs and Google Classroom, which add even more functionality. Kaizena (http://kaizena.com) is an exciting example that provides a means for teachers to give students audio comments on work submitted through Google Classroom—making feedback both faster to deliver *and* more personal for recipients.

There's a simple lesson here: our goal with feedforward strategies shouldn't be to just show students examples of high-quality work before they get started on an assignment. Instead, our goal with feedforward strategies should be to encourage students *to work alongside* examples of high-quality work as they refine and revise their own products. Digital tools like Google Docs and Google Classroom make that possible.

Conclusion

Have you figured out how the feedforward strategies in this chapter are fundamentally different from the feedback strategies in traditional classrooms? Instead of reviewing first drafts or final products looking for places where students failed to meet expectations, teachers using High and Low Comparison tasks, Revise It Once / Revise It Again activities, and Need to Have / Nice to Have activities invest real time and energy into helping students fully understand expectations before they create first drafts and final copies. The goal isn't to find evidence of all the places where students were wrong; the goal is to help students learn to be right by exploring examples of accomplishment before work even begins (Goldsmith, 2002).

What makes High and Low Comparison tasks, Revise It Once / Revise It Again activities, and Need to Have / Nice to Have activities even more powerful is that they focus on the characteristics of *accomplished work* instead of on the characteristics of *accomplished workers*. That's an essential distinction in classrooms moving from a culture of grading to a culture of feedback, because it reminds students that the information gathered during an instructional cycle isn't about making judgments—it is about driving growth. By using exemplars to deliver information about the characteristics of accomplishment, feedforward strategies like High and Low Comparison tasks, Revise It Once / Revise It Again activities, and Need to Have / Nice to Have activities strip away the feelings of defensiveness and shame that sometimes come with feedback on the work products students create. That makes learning safer for everyone.

Chapter 3
What Are My Next Steps?

Here's an interesting question: what happens in your classroom when you hand back assignments? If your students are anything like ours, they check their grades and promptly file their papers into binders, recycle bins, or trash cans. That's discouraging, isn't it? We spend long hours and late nights filling margins with comments and covering rubrics with check marks only to see students move on without giving our feedback a second thought.

There are lots of reasons why students don't really care to hear what you have to say about their work. Some have learned to tune out feedback because it has always been too general to be worthwhile. Spend a decade reading vague comments like "Good work," "I like this," "Remember to capitalize proper nouns," and "Don't forget to indent," and you would question the value of teacher comments too. Others tune out feedback because it has always been overwhelming. Being buried under a thousand things left to learn can cripple some students. Most, however, are ready to move on simply because that's the classroom's regular rhythm. Teachers assign tasks, collect papers, and give grades. Students complete work. The student's job is to turn something in. The teacher's job is to score it. Nothing more, nothing less.

Here's another question: when was the last time you passed back an assignment and gave students time to really wrestle with the comments you worked so hard to add to their papers? Chances are that your answer is just as discouraging. Even though we believe in the power of asking students to reflect on where they are versus where they need to be—and even though those practices mirror behaviors progressive employers value in a world where knowing isn't nearly as important as doing—we feel the constant pressure to move forward as fast as possible. Coverage remains our instructional priority and, as a result, we push aside practices that are messy. Less teaching and more feedback may be the key to achieving greater learning (Wiggins, 2012), but more teaching and less feedback is the key to getting through the required curriculum—the only outcome that matters in our test-first-and-ask-questions-later society. Changing this dynamic is the primary focus of this chapter. Our goal is to introduce practical strategies teachers can use to help students recognize that taking action after receiving feedback is the defining characteristic of successful learners.

Moving Forward

Successful learners are constantly reflecting on information they collect—identifying worthy pursuits, defining the characteristics of success, and drawing conclusions about what they must do in order to move forward. These moments of careful introspection, where learners make personal decisions about how to improve, are essential for developing intellectual independence. As John Hattie (2012b) writes, "Feedback at this level fosters the willingness and capability to seek and effectively deal with feedback, to self-assess and self-correct, to attribute success to effort more than to ability, and to develop effective help-seeking skills" (p. 21). Strategies for developing self-assessment, self-correction, and help-seeking skills in students include reflection checklists, unit analysis forms, feedback forms, and next steps reflection sheets.

Reflection Checklists

Reflection checklists serve many of the same functions as rubrics. Both are tools outlining the core traits of proficient performance.

Students can also use both to evaluate their work against grade-level expectations. Reflection checklists, however, only detail the characteristics of accomplished final products, while rubrics describe the full range of performance on assignments—from "task demonstrates no evidence of mastery" to "task demonstrates levels of mastery that exceed expectations." Reflection checklists are more approachable to learners because they have a clear focus on descriptions of mastery— the expectation for *every* learner.

Like most of the strategies in *Creating a Culture of Feedback*, reflection checklists include indicators that teachers can easily observe in student products. As students add check marks to each indicator on a reflection checklist, clear patterns appear in their performance. These patterns help students identify how they can improve their work. Remember that the characteristics of accomplishment on reflection checklists must mirror the same characteristics in the student work shared with learners in the activities in chapter 2. Also, remember that reflection checklists should provide students with an opportunity to state what their next steps will be. See figure 3.1 for an example.

Reflection Checklists: Paper Towel Lab

Use the following checklists to evaluate the hypothesis, table, bar graph, and conclusion from our paper towel lab. Check off the statements that best describe your work. Consider having a peer rate your work too.

Hypothesis	Table	Bar Graph	Conclusion
☐ My hypothesis is written in an "If, then, because" format.	☐ My table has a title that accurately explains what we were trying to learn in our lab.	☐ My graph has a title that accurately explains what we were trying to learn in our lab.	☐ My conclusion starts with a summary of my results.
Suggestions for improvement:			

Figure 3.1: Sample reflection checklists.

Visit **go.SolutionTree.com/assessment** *for a free reproducible version of this figure.*

Unit Analysis Forms

Students can also use unit analysis forms for reflection at the end of an instructional cycle. Unit analysis forms—an idea built on Stiggins and Chappuis's (2005) student-involved assessment practices—include three essential components: (1) a list of outcomes that students are expected to master during the unit, (2) a list of specific tasks students complete during the unit (quiz questions, test questions, and classroom assignments) that they can use as evidence of mastery, and (3) an opportunity for students to reflect on the progress they have made over the course of a unit. (See figure 3.2.)

Unit analysis forms should also ask learners to decide whether their struggles result from conceptual errors or simple mistakes. Fisher and Frey (2012) write:

> Typically, we make mistakes through lack of attention. But once they are pointed out to us, we immediately recognize them and usually know the corrective action to take. . . . Errors, on the other hand, occur because of lack of knowledge. Even when alerted, the learner isn't quite sure what to do to fix the problem. (p. 44)

Unit analysis forms are powerful tools for helping students seek and effectively deal with feedback, primarily because they make it possible to spot differing levels of mastery across all the outcomes covered within a unit. That means students can see exactly which outcomes they have mastered and which outcomes they continue to wrestle with. For students who struggle, this kind of targeted feedback can be a source of encouragement. Instead of feeling like failures after earning a low score, they are likely to spot concepts and skills they successfully mastered. More important, unit analysis forms can help struggling learners and their teachers be more efficient, spending time revisiting genuine errors instead of wasting time correcting simple mistakes (Fisher & Frey, 2012). This kind of outcome-specific feedback is typically missing in classrooms that give single grades for tasks or tests covering multiple topics or learning targets.

Unit Analysis Form: Scientific Method

Look back over your lithosphere test for patterns in the questions that you got right and that you got wrong. Then, check your unit overview sheets and returned papers to see the kinds of scores you earned on other classroom assignments. Finally, sort each learning target into one of three categories—(1) I've mastered these targets, (2) I need a quick review of these targets, or (3) These targets are still really hard for me.

Learning Targets	Test Questions (Circle questions you got wrong.)
1. I can identify and create questions and hypotheses through scientific investigations.	Questions 2, 3, 4, 7, 13
2. I can develop a set of appropriate procedures to test any question.	Questions 1, 5, 6, 8, 11, 14, 15, 16, 17
Your Reflections	
I've Mastered These Targets These are targets where you answered every question correctly or did really well on other classroom assignments.	
I Need a Quick Review of These Targets These are targets where you made simple mistakes when answering questions incorrectly or working on other classroom assignments.	
These Targets Are Still Really Hard for Me These are targets where you answered the majority of questions incorrectly or really struggled on other classroom assignments.	
Final Thoughts	

Source: Adapted from Stiggins & Chappuis, 2005.

Figure 3.2: Sample unit analysis form.

*Visit **go.SolutionTree.com/assessment** for a free reproducible version of this figure.*

Feedback Forms

The challenge of using reflection checklists and unit analysis forms in isolation is that they can inadvertently focus students on individual qualities instead of the overall quality of a work product. As a result, students can fixate on whether discrete expectations appear in their work and forget that discrete expectations work together as a demonstration of mastery (Sadler, 2002). One strategy to encourage students to look beyond individual qualities when considering their level of mastery is to use feedback forms, an adaptation of Chappuis's (2012) assessment dialogue forms. Feedback forms ask students to (1) reflect on their own work, (2) get feedback from a teacher or a peer, and (3) identify changes that they can make to improve their final products. (See figure 3.3 for an example.)

Feedback Form

Please take a few minutes to think through the strengths and weaknesses you exhibited during our classroom activity.

What I Think About My Work

The things that I have done well are:

This is helpful because:

The things that I could improve are:

This needs to change because:

What I still don't understand how to do or what I need more help with:

Feedback From a Teacher or a Peer

The things that you have done well are:

The things that you could improve are:

What Will I Do Next?

Before I turn in my work, I am going to:

This will improve my work because:

Source: Adapted from Chappuis, 2012.

Figure 3.3: Sample feedback form.

*Visit **go.SolutionTree.com/assessment** for a free reproducible version of this figure.*

Feedback forms encourage students to look more comprehensively at their work. Instead of listing specific criteria or pointing students to specific pieces of evidence they can use as proof of mastery, feedback forms encourage students to use what they already know about accomplished performance in order to draw conclusions about their learning. Essentially, feedback forms remove some of the scaffolding that both reflection checklists and unit analysis forms provide, requiring students to do more thinking. Simple sentence starters like "What I've done well is" and "This is helpful because" point students to the strengths in their work, while sentence starters like "Things I could improve on are" and "What I still don't understand how to do is" suggest that every product or performance can be improved. Finally, sentence starters like "Before I turn in my work, I am going to" and "This will improve my work because" encourage students to act with intentionality after receiving feedback.

Next Steps Reflection Sheets

A similar strategy for encouraging students to look beyond individual qualities when considering their level of mastery is to use next steps reflection sheets, which ask students to articulate the outcomes they are trying to master during an instructional cycle, collect formal and informal evidence of their learning, and determine actions they can take to continue moving forward. Next steps reflection sheets also include simple questions that encourage students to think about their progress, which are best answered in conversations with side partners. See figure 3.4 (page 44) for an example.

For struggling learners, consider creating a highly scripted next steps reflection sheet, like the "Next Steps: Matter Unit." Visit **go.SolutionTree.com/assessment** to download this free reproducible. Notice that it is a highly scripted reflection sheet for a sixth-grade unit on matter that teachers could use with students who need more explicit scaffolding. Teachers detail essential outcomes, evidence of mastery, and logical next steps in advance, making it easier for

Where Am I Going? What essential content and skills do I need to master during this unit? What key questions have I been wrestling with?	How Am I Doing? What evidence can I collect to track my progress toward mastering essential content and skills?	What Are My Next Steps? What steps do I need to take in order to continue my learning?
☐ Can I name the measurable properties of matter? ☐ Can I accurately measure the mass, volume, and density of a solid and a liquid?	☐ Score on matter unit vocabulary test: ☐ Score on states of matter research project:	☐ Review classroom EDpuzzle tutorials on the following topics: ☐ Meet with a peer tutor during intervention period.
Reflection Questions to Answer With a Partner		
What do you already know about the content or skills we are studying?	What patterns do you see in the evidence that you have been collecting about your learning?	How would you rate your overall mastery of the essential content or skills in this unit? Why?

Figure 3.4: Sample next steps reflection sheet.

*Visit **go.SolutionTree.com/assessment** for a free reproducible version of this figure.*

students to successfully reflect on their learning. Over time, teachers interested in reinforcing the core behaviors of independent, action-oriented learners can remove this scaffolding by handing out a blank next steps reflection sheet and asking students to generate lists of expected outcomes, evidence of mastery, and next steps without teacher support.

Integrating reflection checklists, unit analysis forms, feedback forms, and next steps reflection sheets into your instruction is an important step toward giving students responsibility for identifying outcomes, monitoring progress, and setting goals—all critical behaviors in classrooms moving from a culture of grading to a culture of feedback.

Improving Peer Feedback

One of the best ways to ensure that classrooms become places where meaningful feedback is delivered every day is to help students become better at giving feedback to—and receiving feedback from—their peers. Outside of simply increasing the amount of information available to learners, giving and receiving peer feedback is powerful because, like reflection activities, students can be the primary authorities on their own progress.

Peer feedback also allows students to be intellectually vulnerable in front of one another and to recognize that they can rely on classmates for support. Finally, peer feedback provides students with multiple opportunities to spot success criteria in age-appropriate sample work, building confidence in their ability to accurately pinpoint strengths and weaknesses in their own final products (Nuthall, 2007). But make no mistake: peer feedback can be intimidating to learners. After years of seeing teachers blend feedback with evaluation, learners often slip into unhealthy patterns of using peer feedback as an opportunity to pass judgment on one another.

In fact, the first step toward turning peer feedback into a safe, productive learning experience for students is to clearly highlight the difference between observations and evaluations—a distinction most students will not automatically understand. Observations are unbiased and communicate tangible characteristics that others can see in the same way, while evaluations include subjective interpretations that are often opinion based. Observations are also quicker to give and to receive because they don't require lengthy justifications. Finally, observations eliminate the asymmetrical power dynamic that some students encounter during peer feedback (Price, Handley, Millar, & O'Donovan, 2010). Because the student giving feedback is not judging or advising future action but rather sharing information as objectively as possible, the student receiving feedback doesn't feel inferior—increasing the likelihood that any information shared will result in action. (See table 3.1, page 46, for examples of observation versus evaluation.)

Table 3.1: Observation Versus Evaluation

	Observation	**Evaluation**
Objectivity	Can be a simple, unbiased view of the behavior	Includes a value judgment, which is often opinion based and problematic for peers
Time and Effort	Is quick and simple for the observer and the one being observed	Lengthy due to explanation of the rating
Impact	Allows for rapid response and small readjustments	Often ignored because the evaluator lacks the respect of the one being evaluated
Next Steps	Decided by the one being observed, providing agency and ownership	Often the final step without reflection or iteration
Example	"Jimmy, I noticed that the first letter of your second sentence is lowercase. That made it difficult for me to tell when the first sentence ended."	"Jimmy, your first paragraph is below standard. The first letter of each sentence should have been capitalized."

One of the best examples of students making observations instead of giving evaluations is the story of Austin's butterfly (http://bit .ly/msdbutterfly; EL Education, 2012). In this video, Ron Berger of EL Education, works with students at Presumpscot Elementary School in Portland, Maine, who are comparing a photograph of a butterfly to a scientific illustration that a first grader named Austin created. Throughout the video, Berger encourages the students to offer specific suggestions about both the shape and coloration of the butterfly's wings. Differences between Austin's work and the photograph are easy to spot, making it possible for every student to successfully practice giving feedback in the form of observations. More important, by highlighting Austin's improvements from revision to revision, Berger provides students with evidence that descriptive feedback really can have a positive impact on students' work (EL Education, 2012).

What makes Berger's lesson so powerful is that any teacher can easily replicate it. All that you need is a task where students create a product based on an exemplar. Like Austin's butterfly, you could have students create a scientific illustration. You could also have students replicate a diagram, map, or photograph. Once students have finished first drafts, pair them with partners to give and receive feedback. Consider sharing simple sentence starters to guide the process. A list of four or five opening phrases that lead into observations can ensure that these early feedback opportunities build confidence in both the givers and receivers of feedback. Consider the following.

- "I noticed that _____"
- "I wonder if _____"
- "What if you _____"
- "It seems to me that _____"
- "This looks different than the original because _____"
- "I'm not sure that _____"

Finish the task by asking students to make revisions to their original drafts based on their partners' observations. Doing so serves as a reminder that feedback is supposed to lead to action.

As students grow more comfortable with observations as a viable form of peer feedback, ask them to tackle more complex and less concrete tasks. Classrooms can apply the same process to any work product—mathematics-problem solutions, student essays, presentations, or performances—in any subject area. Each new opportunity for peers to share nonjudgmental information strengthens the kind of positive classroom climate where learners can genuinely thrive alongside one another.

Using Digital Tools to Help Students Understand Their Next Steps

The most obvious type of feedback that students receive is results from formal assessments. Sadly, however, time constraints often cause teachers to skip the essential epilogue to most tests and quizzes: chances for students to look at results, reflect on their mastery of individual learning targets, and identify gaps in their growth. As Susan M. Brookhart (2012), a research associate at the Center for Advancing the Study of Teaching and Learning, writes, "Feedback can't be left hanging. It can't work if students don't have an immediate opportunity to use it" (p. 27). Fortunately, tech tools can help teachers design time-friendly reflection opportunities for classroom assessments.

One of the best tools for giving students chances to plan for their own improvement is Socrative (www.socrative.com). Socrative is a free tool that allows teachers to deliver short, formative assessments and to give students instant feedback. Socrative has several advantages over traditional quizzes and other online assessment services. Perhaps most important, the interface is entirely web based, with no application to install on any system (desktop, laptop, tablet, or smartphone) for either the teacher or student. That means Socrative works no matter what kind of technology is available. Have a class set of iPads? Using Chromebooks with your students? Making due with a hodgepodge collection of devices you have acquired over time? Socrative will work. Second, students do not need usernames and passwords to use Socrative; users sign in with a unique classroom code and their names at the start of an assessment. By eliminating two of the most common barriers to the efficient use of digital tools in classrooms—ensuring that their service works regardless of device and allowing students to sign in without usernames and passwords—Socrative has positioned itself as a tool to provide instant feedback in *any* classroom *every* day.

While using Socrative, students can see their scores immediately or at the end of an assessment, and teachers can share graphs of student responses with the entire class. Questions can include images, making it possible to integrate digital photographs of sample work into Socrative assessments, and students can answer in short sentences or paragraphs, allowing for assessments that include more than just multiple-choice questions. Result reports are color-coded to highlight right and wrong answers, making it possible to quickly spot patterns in student mastery, and teachers can store them within Socrative or export them as spreadsheets. Teachers can also share Socrative quizzes with other teachers—an important feature for collaborative teams who are creating common formative assessments. For extra benefit, consider pairing Socrative with the unit overview sheets from chapter 1 by adding a running log page to the Your Proof section, where students can record scores on daily Socrative warm-up exercises and track the small steps they are taking toward mastering essential outcomes.

Another tool that can help students to plan for improvement is MasteryConnect (www.masteryconnect.com). MasteryConnect is an online assessment tool that offers many ways for students to take traditional assessments. Using preprinted bubble sheets, teachers can administer assessments with pencil and paper and automatically score them by taking a photo with the camera on any laptop, tablet, or smartphone using a free web browser plugin or mobile app. Students can also use any web browser or the MasteryConnect app to take assessments. The real beauty of MasteryConnect is in the way that it displays student learning. Teachers tag assessment questions with the curriculum standard they are measuring, allowing MasteryConnect to sort and report results *by student* and *by standard* in a color-coded grid called the Mastery Tracker. With one quick glance, teachers can see which targets are the trickiest and which students need more help.

Students with email addresses can access their MasteryConnect assessment data online, making it possible to track performance independent of their teachers. They can see their most recent level of mastery for each learning target and access additional study resources—online tutorials, classroom handouts, extra problem sets, or inquiry questions—for every standard. As with daily Socrative data, students can plot MasteryConnect results in their notebooks or on their unit overview sheets—creating a mastery hub that can serve as an important starting point for drawing conclusions about next steps worth taking.

MasteryConnect data become especially powerful, however, when teachers pair them with differentiated review activities in the classroom. One strategy for structuring differentiated review is the activity Secret Agent Code Name. The first step in Secret Agent Code Name is for students to log in to MasteryConnect and record their individual level of mastery from the Mastery Tracker—remediation (red), near mastery (yellow), or mastery (green)—for each standard in a unit of study. Doing so reminds students that it is entirely possible to master some objectives and struggle with others during an instructional cycle. A student might be at the remediation level (red) for one target, near mastery (yellow) for another, and mastery (green) for a third learning target in the same unit.

Next, students use a chart to convert the colors representing their mastery levels on each learning target into a playful secret agent code name. (See figure 3.5.)

Each word in a secret agent code name points students to specific stations around the classroom with unique review, extra practice, or extension tasks for the learning targets covered during a unit. For example, a student who is near mastery in targets A and B but in need of remediation for target C, might have Fuzzy Blue Platypus as a secret agent code name. Over the course of one or two class periods, that student would complete the tasks at the Fuzzy station, Blue station, and Platypus station in the classroom.

Learning Target	Your Level of Mastery (Collected from MasteryConnect)	Your Code Word (Circle.)
Learning Target A I can add two fractions with different denominators.	Remediation (red)	Hairy
	Near Mastery (yellow)	Fuzzy
	Mastery (green)	Pointy
Learning Target B I can subtract two fractions with different denominators.	Remediation (red)	Pink
	Near Mastery (yellow)	Blue
	Mastery (green)	Purple
Learning Target C I can solve word problems that involve fractions with different denominators.	Remediation (red)	Platypus
	Near Mastery (yellow)	Snake
	Mastery (green)	Bear
Your secret agent code name: Combine all three circled words into one unique animal. Example: Fuzzy Blue Platypus!		

Figure 3.5: Secret Agent Code Name chart for unit on fractions.

*Visit **go.SolutionTree.com/assessment** for a free reproducible version of this figure.*

The stations can include tasks to help students review important concepts, such as making sets of vocabulary flashcards, watching target-specific videos on the web, designing tutorials classmates in need of extra help can use, working with peer tutors to get feedback on important assignments, playing review games, or meeting with the teacher for additional instruction. The goal of Secret Agent Code Name is to provide a customized review experience for individual students based on strengths and weaknesses. Students appreciate the academic privacy that comes from having a secret agent code name and love that the tasks are not one size fits all—and teachers free themselves from the front of the classroom and are then able to move around, monitor student work, and provide guidance as needed.

Conclusion

Can you see what's *not* happening in any of the activities highlighted in this chapter? Regardless of the strategy, teachers are not handing out suggestions to students but rather providing opportunities for students to discover the characteristics of a successful work product on their own. Each opportunity serves as proof to students that there *are* standards of success for any task—and that they *can* understand, recognize, and replicate those standards.

Wiliam (2015) describes this shift as turning feedback into detective work, and it requires a willingness to reimagine the role that both teachers and students play in the learning process. Instead of spending hours filling papers with well-intentioned comments, teachers who are turning feedback into detective work spend hours designing opportunities for students to identify and interpret evidence of learning. Instead of waiting for information from teachers, students think carefully about the task, compare their work against exemplars of success, and draw conclusions about next steps based on an understanding of their own strengths and weaknesses. The goal isn't to simply *give* students feedback. It is to give students opportunities to practice making decisions about what's next based on feedback that they *gather* on their own.

Conclusion

No matter how long you have been teaching, chances are that at some point, you have been frustrated with students who seem completely indifferent to their own success. Some disrupt class constantly. Others want nothing more than to blend in and disappear. Regardless, their actions convinced you that they just didn't *want* to do better in school. Look a little closer, though, and you are likely to find that the most indifferent students bear a stronger resemblance to veteran boxers than unmotivated slackers. Their academic numbness is a result of years of taking too many punches. Apathy becomes a coping strategy when you are forced to constantly protect yourself from a relentless stream of messages that you aren't measuring up—a process that repeats itself over and over again for students who struggle in school.

Josue was one of those students. He rarely felt successful and decided early on that the best way to avoid struggling in front of his middle school peers was to crack jokes and make his classmates laugh. "I wasn't going to get it," he said. "And if I wasn't going to get it, I figured I'd just have some fun" (J. Hernandez, personal communication, April 20, 2016). Josue went on to explain that he had stopped trying because he was convinced he had learned all the "school stuff" that he could. "I learn my own stuff fine," he said. "But not school stuff" (J. Hernandez, personal communication, April 20, 2016). To Josue, there was simply no moving forward. To his teachers, he just didn't seem to care.

Still, we know from years of experience and dozens of research studies that there *is* a way forward for students like Josue. Integrating indifferent students back into the learning environment starts when we create the kinds of classrooms where *all students* can see evidence that they are capable of learning and where *all students* understand that they are moving forward even if they haven't achieved mastery in the moment (Stiggins & Chappuis, 2005). Carol Dweck (2014) calls this "luxuriating in the power of yet" rather than being "gripped in the tyranny of now." We call this moving from a culture of grading to a culture of feedback, and it is an essential first step toward developing confident, self-directed learners.

Make no mistake, however: moving from a culture of grading to a culture of feedback won't be easy, no matter how motivated you are. That's because grades play so many roles in our schools—some of which contradict one another, and others which run contrary to the goal of measuring mastery and encouraging learners. Parents expect grades to tell them what their child has learned while simultaneously communicating information about work ethic, organizational skills, and attention levels in class. Schools use grades to determine athletic eligibility, class rankings, and who graduates and who doesn't. College admissions officers, by extension, rely in some measure on grades to make acceptance decisions. In many ways, these simple numbers and letters have become more important than the learning they are supposed to represent.

But the time is right for change—and outside pressure for something better is coming from a surprising source: businesses who are redefining the criteria used to make hiring decisions, a trend that started with the tech firms of Silicon Valley. Need proof? Then consider that high marks from prestigious universities mean almost nothing to Laszlo Bock, senior vice president for people operations at Google, who is convinced that grade point averages and test scores are worthless tools for identifying worthy applicants:

> I think academic environments are artificial environments. People who succeed there are sort of finely trained, they're conditioned to succeed in that environment. One of my own frustrations when I was in

> college and grad school is that you knew the professor
> was looking for a specific answer. You could figure that
> out, but it's much more interesting to solve problems
> where there isn't an obvious answer. You want people
> who like figuring out stuff where there is no obvious
> answer. (as cited in Bryant, 2013)

So what *is* Bock looking for in an employee? Most important, new hires at Google have to demonstrate strong cognitive skills—the ability to learn in the moment and to find meaning in seemingly unrelated bits of information (Friedman, 2014). Google also values emergent leadership—recognizing a problem and willingly stepping forward to move a team toward a resolution—and intellectual humility. Bock argues:

> Successful, bright people rarely experience failure,
> and so they don't learn how to learn from that fail-
> ure. They, instead, commit the fundamental attribution
> error, which is if something good happens, it's because
> I'm a genius. If something bad happens, it's because
> someone's an idiot, or I didn't get the resources, or the
> market moved. (as cited in Friedman, 2014)

The least important criteria in Google's hiring decisions: expertise (Friedman, 2014).

Traditional indicators of expertise are also becoming less important in the hiring decisions of widely recognized companies in more traditional fields. Take the U.K. office of Ernst and Young—one of the world's largest accounting firms. In August 2015, it stopped requiring college degrees for entry-level positions, instead relying on skill surveys to identify candidates with potential. Their internal studies "found no evidence to conclude that previous success in higher education correlated with future success in subsequent professional qualifications undertaken" (Ernst and Young Global Limited, 2015). Similarly, publisher Penguin Random House removed degree requirements and grade-point-average minimums from its U.K. hiring materials in early 2016 (Sherriff, 2016). Like Ernst and Young, Penguin Random House saw no real connection between holding a college degree and being successful in the workplace. More important, Penguin Random House wanted to extend opportunities to students who hadn't been successful by traditional metrics, ensuring that "academic qualifications will no longer act as a barrier to talented people getting a foot in the door to publishing" (Sherriff, 2016).

Can you see the potential and the promise in these actions? If highly respected employers stop putting a premium on grades and start prioritizing the skills that define the most adept learners in their hiring decisions, maybe our schools will *finally* follow suit and prioritize those same skills in the work that we do with students. But why wait for these changes to trickle down into classrooms? Regardless of the role you fill, there are approachable steps to take right now to create the learning spaces students deserve, including starting conversations with parents and students about the difference between grading and feedback, completing a feedback inventory to surface assumptions about grading and feedback, and integrating opportunities for self-assessment into the work you do with parents and practitioners.

Starting Conversations With Parents and Students About the Difference Between Grading and Feedback

One barrier preventing schools from creating the learning spaces students deserve is the core beliefs that parents, practitioners, principals, and policymakers hold about grading and feedback in schools. Traditional notions—ranking and sorting students, defining accomplishment by earning the highest marks, using grades as tools for motivating learners, and delivering feedback at the end of an instructional cycle—have defined schools for the better part of a century. Little about our practices will change if our most important stakeholders continue to hold on to long-standing assumptions about the role that grades and feedback should play in learners' lives.

Progressive educators need to start conversations with both parents and students about the fundamental differences between grading and feedback. To begin that work, ask parents and students to complete the "Classroom Feedback Survey: Parents" and "Classroom Feedback Survey: Students" at **go.SolutionTree.com/assessment**, which will give you a better sense of what the most important stakeholders in your school population currently believe about grading and feedback. You can use the information gathered to craft and deliver messages—during parent nights, school communications, and classroom conversations—that build awareness about the role that meaningful feedback can play in preparing students for modern workplace demands.

Completing a Feedback Inventory to Surface Assumptions About Grading and Feedback

Challenging traditional assumptions and beliefs about grading and feedback in schools depends on more than starting conversations with parents and students, however. Change can only begin when we revise our instructional practices. If we want to develop learners who can demonstrate cognitive ability, emergent leadership, and intellectual humility on the fly—the skills that Google prioritizes above individual expertise—we must encourage each other to rethink the role students play in the feedback process.

To start that work, consider completing—or asking the teachers that you work with to complete—the "Feedback Practice Inventory" at **go.SolutionTree.com/assessment**, which will help surface the common grading and feedback patterns that govern professional choices in your classrooms, learning teams, and schools. It will also help to identify how best to move from a culture of grading to a culture of feedback.

Integrating Opportunities for Self-Assessment Into the Work You Do With Parents and Practitioners

Until both teachers and parents have firsthand experiences with what using feedback to cause thinking or turning feedback into a fulcrum for continued growth looks like in action, they will struggle to fully support efforts to move from a culture of grading to a culture of feedback.

So how can you give teachers and parents those firsthand experiences? A simple first step would be to turn agendas for every meeting—faculty meetings, parent nights, professional development sessions, and Parent-Teacher Association (PTA) gatherings—into unit overview sheets that describe essential outcomes in approachable language. Then, integrate regular opportunities for self-assessment into your presentations. Ask participants to rate their understanding of key outcomes at the beginning of your session, give them chances to share their ratings with partners throughout your session, and remind them to change their ratings at the end of the session. These exercises remind everyone that the best feedback is active and learner centered, not passive and teacher centered. Visit **go.SolutionTree .com/assessment** to find reproducibles of staff development and parent overview sheets to use as agendas for faculty meetings or parent nights.

Shifting Our Thinking

In December 2014, school leadership expert Scott McLeod (2014) made the case that our schools, which continue, in many cases, to define success by the amount of content that students can memorize, are leaving our students poorly prepared for the work they will tackle after graduation: "Somehow, we have to shift our schools' overwhelming emphasis on low-level knowledge work into something that better meets our graduates' needs to navigate vastly different information and economic spaces."

Together we can begin to shift our schools from low-level knowledge work into something better by prioritizing feedback over grading in our instructional practices. Every time your students have opportunities to think about where they are going, how they are doing, and which steps to take next, they further realize they *can* accomplish powerful things on their own. In a world where mastering content and developing expertise aren't nearly as important as they once were, no single message could be more important to send.

References

Azzam, A. M. (2007). Special report: Why students drop out. *Educational Leadership, 64*(7), 91–93. Accessed at www.ascd.org /publications/educational-leadership/apr07/vol64/num07/Why -Students-Drop-Out.aspx on January 3, 2015.

Brookhart, S. M. (2012). Preventing feedback fizzle. *Educational Leadership, 70*(1), 24–29.

Bryant, A. (2013, June 19). In head-hunting, big data may not be such a big deal. *New York Times.* Accessed at www.nytimes.com /2013/06/20/business/in-head-hunting-big-data-may-not-be -such-a-big-deal.html on February 4, 2016.

Busteed, B. (2013, January 7). *The school cliff: Student engagement drops with each school year* [Blog post]. Accessed at www.gallup .com/opinion/gallup/170525/school-cliff-student-engagement -drops-school-year.aspx on October 10, 2014.

Chappuis, J. (2012). "How am I doing?" *Educational Leadership, 70*(1), 36–41.

Cohen, J. F. W., Richardson, S., Parker, E., Catalano, P. J., & Rimm, E. B. (2014). Impact of the new U.S. Department of Agriculture School Meal Standards on food selection, consumption, and waste. *American Journal of Preventive Medicine, 46*(4), 388–394.

Dweck, C. (2014, November). *The power of believing that you can improve* [Video file]. Accessed at www.ted.com/talks/carol _dweck_the_power_of_believing_that_you_can_improve? language=en on February 4, 2016.

EL Education. (2012, March 9). *Austin's butterfly: Building excellence in student work* [Video file]. Accessed at https://vimeo.com /38247060 on February 4, 2016.

Ernst and Young Global Limited. (2015). *EY transforms its recruitment selection process for graduates, undergraduates and school leavers* [Press release]. Accessed at www.ey.com/UK/en /Newsroom/News-releases/15-08-03---EY-transforms-its -recruitment-selection-process-for-graduates-undergraduates -and-school-leavers on February 4, 2016.

Fisher, D., & Frey, N. (2012). Making time for feedback. *Educational Leadership, 70*(1), 42–46.

Fisher, D., & Frey, N. (2014). *Checking for understanding: Formative assessment techniques for your classroom* (2nd ed.) [Kindle version]. Alexandria, VA: Association for Supervision and Curriculum Development.

Friedman, T. L. (2014, February 22). How to get a job at Google. *New York Times.* Accessed at www.nytimes.com/2014/02/23 /opinion/sunday/friedman-how-to-get-a-job-at-google.html on February 4, 2016.

Goldsmith, M. (2002). *Try feedforward instead of feedback.* Accessed at www.marshallgoldsmithlibrary.com/cim/articles_display.php ?aid=110 on April 1, 2016.

Guskey, T. R. (2009). Grading policies that work against standards . . . and how to fix them. In T. R. Guskey (Ed.), *Practical solutions for serious problems in standards-based grading* (pp. 9–26). Thousand Oaks, CA: Corwin Press.

Hart Research Associates. (2015). *Falling short? College learning and career success—Selected findings from online surveys of employers and college students conducted on behalf of the Association of American Colleges and Universities.* Washington, DC: Author.

Hattie, J. (2009). *Visible learning: A synthesis of over 800 meta-analyses relating to achievement.* London: Routledge.

Hattie, J. (2012a). Feedback in schools. In R. M. Sutton, M. J. Hornsey, & K. M. Douglas (Eds.), *Feedback: The communication of praise, criticism and advice* (pp. 265–278). New York: Lang.

Hattie, J. (2012b). Know thy impact. *Educational Leadership*, *70*(1), 18–23.

Marzano, R. J. (2003). *What works in schools: Translating research into action*. Alexandria, VA: Association for Supervision and Curriculum Development.

Mattos, M., DuFour, R., DuFour, R., Eaker, R., & Many, T. W. (2016). *Concise answers to frequently asked questions about Professional Learning Communities at Work*. Bloomington, IN: Solution Tree Press.

McLeod, S. (2014, December 12). *We need schools to be different* [Blog post]. Accessed at www.dangerouslyirrelevant.org/2014/12/we -need-schools-to-be-different.html on January 3, 2015.

National Association of Colleges and Employers. (2014, November). *Job outlook 2015* [Survey]. Bethlehem, PA: Author.

Nuthall, G. (2007). *The hidden lives of learners*. Wellington, New Zealand: NZCER Press.

Papert, S. (1998, June 2). *Child power: Keys to the new learning of the digital century* [Speech]. Accessed at www.papert.org/articles /Childpower.html on May 19, 2016.

Price, M., Handley, K., Millar, J. & O'Donovan, B. (2010). Feedback: All that effort, but what is the effect? *Assessment and Evaluation in Higher Education*, *35*(3), 277–289.

Reeves, D. (2002). *The leader's guide to standards: A blueprint for educational equity and excellence*. San Francisco: Jossey-Bass.

Sadler, D. R. (1998). Formative assessment: Revisiting the territory. *Assessment in Education*, *5*(1), 77–84.

Sadler, D. R. (2002). Ah! . . . so that's 'quality.' In P. Schwartz & G. Webb (Eds)., *Assessment: Case studies, experience, and practice from higher education* (pp. 130–136). London: Kogan Page.

Sherriff, L. (2016, January 18). Penguin Random House Publishers has just announced it's scrapping degree requirements for its jobs. *Huffington Post United Kingdom.* Accessed at www.huffingtonpost .co.uk/2016/01/18/penguins-random-house-scrapping-degree -requirements-jobs_n_9007288.html on May 19, 2016.

Slattery, I. (Producer), & Weimberg, G. (Directors). (2012). *Keep it or junk it: A student-run lesson* [Video file]. Accessed at www .teachingchannel.org/videos/student-run-lesson on July 31, 2016.

Stiggins, R., Arter, J., Chappuis, J., & Chappuis, S. (2004). *Classroom assessment for student learning: Doing it right—using it well.* Portland, OR: Assessment Training Institute.

Stiggins, R., & Chappuis, J. (2005). Using student-involved classroom assessment to close achievement gaps. *Theory Into Practice, 44*(1), 11–18.

Taub-Dix, B. (2014). *Coming to a school lunch tray near you.* Accessed at http://health.usnews.com/health-news/blogs/eat-run /2014/08/21/coming-to-a-school-lunch-tray-near-you on May 20, 2016.

Wiggins, G. (2012). Seven keys to effective feedback. *Educational Leadership, 70*(1), 10–16.

Wiliam, D. (2011). *Embedded formative assessment* [Kindle version]. Bloomington, IN: Solution Tree Press.

Wiliam, D. [dylanwiliam]. (2015, November 22). Or, to put it another way, "Make feedback into detective work." [Tweet]. Accessed at https://twitter.com/dylanwiliam/status/66863 5191531958272 on May 19, 2016.

Solutions for Creating the Learning Spaces Students Deserve

Solutions Series: Solutions for Creating the Learning Spaces Students Deserve reimagines the norms defining K–12 education. In a short, reader-friendly format, these books challenge traditional thinking about schooling and encourage readers to question their beliefs about what real teaching and learning look like in action.

Creating a Culture of Feedback
William M. Ferriter and Paul J. Cancellieri
BKF731

Embracing a Culture of Joy
Dean Shareski
BKF730

Making Learning Flow
John Spencer
BKF733

Reimagining Literacy Through Global Collaboration
Pernille Ripp
BKF732

" Excellent engagement
in what truly matters
in **assessment**.

Great examples! "

PD Services

Our experts draw from decades of research and their own experiences to bring you practical strategies for designing and implementing quality assessments. You can choose from a range of customizable services, from a one-day overview to a multiyear process.

Book your assessment PD today!
888.763.9045

Solution Tree